S

OCEANS OF THE WORLD

THE ARCTIC OCEAN

A MyReportLinks.com Book

DOREEN GONZALES

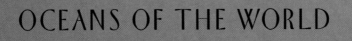

MyReportLinks.com Books
an imprint of
Enslow Publishers, Inc. E
Box 398, 40 Industrial Road
Berkeley Heights, NJ 07922
USA

MyReportLinks.com Books, an imprint of Enslow Publishers, Inc. MyReportLinks®
is a registered trademark of Enslow Publishers, Inc.

Library of Congress Cataloging-in-Publication Data

Gonzalez, Doreen.
  The Arctic Ocean / Doreen Gonzalez.
    p. cm. — (Oceans of the world)
Summary: Describes the physical characteristics, plant and animal life,
explorers, and environmental problems of the world's smallest ocean, the
Arctic. Includes Internet links to web sites related to oceans.
Includes bibliographical references and index.
  ISBN 0-7660-5193-5
  1. Oceanography—Arctic Ocean—Juvenile literature. 2. Arctic
Ocean—Juvenile literature. [1. Arctic Ocean. 2. Oceanography.] I.
Title.
  GC401.G66 2004
  551.46'132—dc22

                                    2003016367

Printed in the United States of America

10 9 8 7 6 5 4 3 2 1

To Our Readers:
Through the purchase of this book, you and your library gain access to the Report Links that specifically back
up this book.
The Publisher will provide access to the Report Links that back up this book and will keep these Report Links
up to date on **www.myreportlinks.com** for three years from the book's first publication date.
We have done our best to make sure all Internet addresses in this book were active and appropriate when we
went to press. However, the author and the Publisher have no control over, and assume no liability for, the
material available on those Internet sites or on other Web sites they may link to.
The usage of the MyReportLinks.com Books Web site is subject to the terms and conditions stated on the
Usage Policy Statement on **www.myreportlinks.com**.
A password may be required to access the Report Links that back up this book. The password is found on the
bottom of page 4 of this book.
Any comments or suggestions can be sent by e-mail to comments@myreportlinks.com or to the address on
the back cover.

Photo Credits: Captain Budd Christman, NOAA, p. 30; Commander Richard Behn, NOAA, p. 12;
© 2002 CyberNatural Software, p. 23; © Corel Corporation, pp. 9, 13, 17, 27, 28, 38, 39, 41, 43;
Defenders of Wildlife, p. 40; GeoAtlas, p. 10; Marsh Youngbluth, NOAA, p. 26; MyReportLinks.com
Books, p. 4; PBS, p. 14; Photos.com, pp. 1, 3; National Oceanic and Atmospheric Association
(NOAA), 21, 36; Rear Admiral Harley D. Nygren, NOAA, p. 19; Smithsonian National Museum of
Natural History, Arctic Studies Center, p. 34; United States Federal Wildlife Service, 31.

Cover Photo: Photodisc

Cover Description: Polar bear in the Arctic Ocean.

Contents

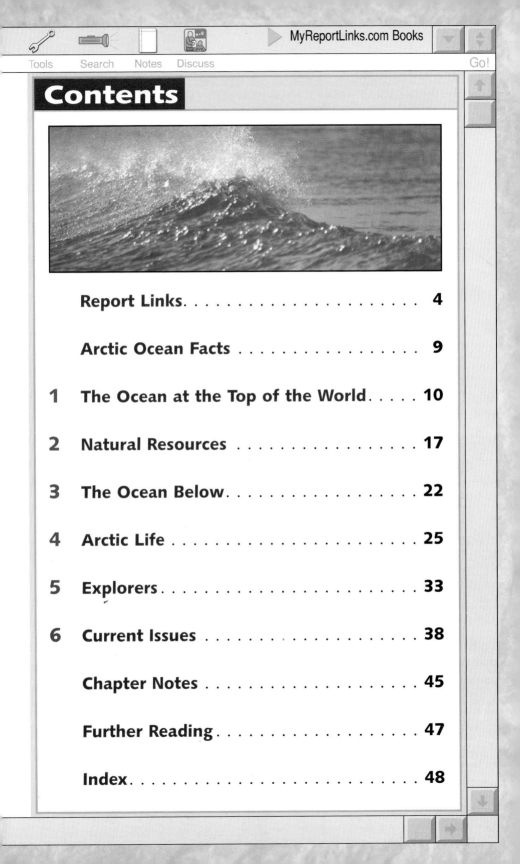

MyReportLinks.com Books
Great Books, Great Links, Great for Research!

The Report Links listed on the following four pages can save you hours of research time by **instantly** bringing you to the best Web sites relating to your report topic.

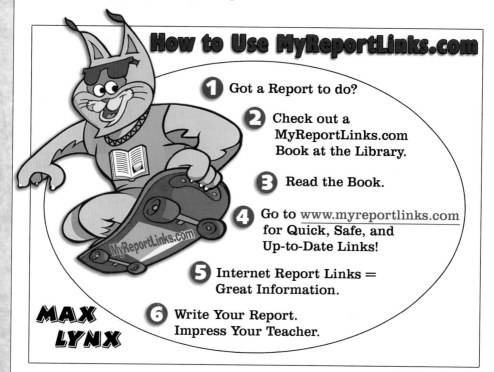

How to Use MyReportLinks.com

1 Got a Report to do?

2 Check out a MyReportLinks.com Book at the Library.

3 Read the Book.

4 Go to www.myreportlinks.com for Quick, Safe, and Up-to-Date Links!

5 Internet Report Links = Great Information.

6 Write Your Report. Impress Your Teacher.

MAX LYNX

The pre-evaluated Web sites are your links to source documents, photographs, illustrations, and maps. They also provide links to dozens—even hundreds—of Web sites about your report subject.

MyReportLinks.com Books and the MyReportLinks.com Web site save you time and make report writing easier than ever!

Please see "To Our Readers" on the copyright page for important information about this book, the MyReportLinks.com Web site, and the Report Links that back up this book. Please enter **OAR8182** if asked for a password.

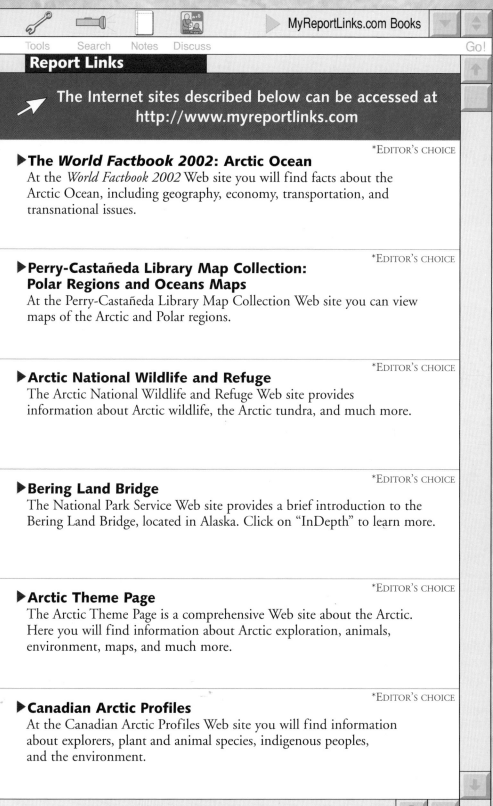

Report Links

The Internet sites described below can be accessed at
http://www.myreportlinks.com

▶**The *World Factbook 2002*: Arctic Ocean**   *EDITOR'S CHOICE
At the *World Factbook 2002* Web site you will find facts about the
Arctic Ocean, including geography, economy, transportation, and
transnational issues.

▶**Perry-Castañeda Library Map Collection:**   *EDITOR'S CHOICE
Polar Regions and Oceans Maps
At the Perry-Castañeda Library Map Collection Web site you can view
maps of the Arctic and Polar regions.

▶**Arctic National Wildlife and Refuge**   *EDITOR'S CHOICE
The Arctic National Wildlife and Refuge Web site provides
information about Arctic wildlife, the Arctic tundra, and much more.

▶**Bering Land Bridge**   *EDITOR'S CHOICE
The National Park Service Web site provides a brief introduction to the
Bering Land Bridge, located in Alaska. Click on "InDepth" to learn more.

▶**Arctic Theme Page**   *EDITOR'S CHOICE
The Arctic Theme Page is a comprehensive Web site about the Arctic.
Here you will find information about Arctic exploration, animals,
environment, maps, and much more.

▶**Canadian Arctic Profiles**   *EDITOR'S CHOICE
At the Canadian Arctic Profiles Web site you will find information
about explorers, plant and animal species, indigenous peoples,
and the environment.

Report Links

**The Internet sites described below can be accessed at
http://www.myreportlinks.com**

▶ **The Arctic: the Ocean, Sea Ice, Icebergs, and Climate**

On this site, you can learn about the Arctic Ocean's environment and climate.
The sinking of the *Titanic*, which was caused by a floating iceberg, is also
briefly discussed.

▶ **Arctic Circle**

At the Arctic Circle Web site you can read articles related to natural resources, history,
culture, and social and environmental issues in the Arctic.

▶ **Arctic Exploration**

Learn about a collaborative effort to explore the Canada Basin in the Arctic.

▶ **Arctic National Wildlife Refuge**

At the Arctic National Wildlife Refuge Web site you will learn about this sanctuary,
the wildlife it contains, and the current problems it is facing.

▶ **The Arctic Oscillation: A Major Impact on our Winter
Weather Patterns**

The Arctic Oscillation Web site contains a brief, illustrated article about how the Arctic
Oscillation impacts weather in the winter.

▶ **Arctic Studies Center**

At the Arctic Studies Web site you can explore Arctic history and culture, and learn
about environmental issues.

▶ ***Aurora Borealis*—The Northern Lights**

At this Web site you will find information about the *Aurora Borealis*, also known as the
northern lights, including what causes this phenomenon.

▶ **Blue Planet Challenge**

At the Blue Planet Challenge Web site you can explore oceans and ocean life. Here you
will find facts about all five oceans, including the Arctic.

Any comments? Contact us: **comments@myreportlinks.com**

Report Links

**The Internet sites described below can be accessed at
http://www.myreportlinks.com**

▶**Creature World: Polar Bear**

At the Creature World Web site you will find a brief profile of the polar bear, one of the Arctic's many residents.

▶**The Cryosphere: Where the World is Frozen**

At the Cryosphere Web site you will learn about the cryosphere, including snow, icebergs, glaciers, and ice shelves.

▶**Global Warming Kids Site**

The Global Warming Kids Site is designed to teach kids about global warming. The site examines what global warming is, how it effects weather and the climate, and much more.

▶**Infoplease.com: Ocean**

Infoplease.com provides an overview of information about the ocean world. Learn about continental shelves, ocean circulation, trenches, and much more.

▶**Lost Liners: *Titanic***

PBS's Lost Liners Web site discusses the *Titanic's* tragic crash into an Arctic iceberg in 1912.

▶**The Marine Mammal Center: Blue Whale**

At the Marine Mammal Center Web site you can find out about the largest mammal on Earth, the blue whale. Blue whales migrate to the Arctic Ocean in the summer.

▶**North of Norway: A Natural Lab**

At the Frontiers Web site there is an article about mud volcanoes that occur in the Arctic.

▶**Oceana**

Oceana, an organization dedicated to protecting the world's oceans, provides information about who they are and what they do.

Report Links

The Internet sites described below can be accessed at http://www.myreportlinks.com

▶**Peary, Robert Edwin**

Encyclopedia.com presents a biography of explorer Robert Edwin Peary. He was the first man to reach the North Pole.

▶**Physical Nutrients and Primary Productivity**

An article about attempts being made to study the Arctic Ocean, and its inhabitants.

▶**Polar Connection**

The Polar Connection Web site offers activities that may help you learn about the Polar region.

▶**Scientists Excited by Arctic Ocean Ridge Finds**

At this *National Geographic* Web site you will find an article about the Arctic Ocean ridge. Find out why scientists are excited about this finding!

▶**Tooth Walkers: Giants of the Arctic Ice**

PBS's *Nature* Web site provides a brief profile of the walrus. It is profiled along with other Arctic creatures.

▶**Towering Mountains**

At this Web site you can learn about the Towering Mountains, including the Lomonosov Ridge and the Alpha-Mendeleev Ridge.

▶**The *World Factbook 2002*: Atlantic Ocean**

The *World Factbook 2002* Web site provides facts about the Atlantic Ocean, including geography, economy, transportation, and transnational issues. The Arctic Ocean and Atlantic Ocean meet at the Greenland Sea.

▶**The *World Factbook 2002*: Pacific Ocean**

At the *World Factbook 2002* Web site you will find facts about the Pacific Ocean, including geography, economy, transportation, and transnational issues. The Arctic Ocean and Pacific Ocean meet at the Bering Strait.

Arctic Ocean Facts

Area
5,427,050 square miles
14,056,000 square
   kilometers

Average Depth
3,953 feet
1,205 meters

Greatest Known Depth
18,456 feet
5,625 meters

Place of Greatest
Know Depth
77°45' North longitude;
175° West latitude

Greatest Distance
About 2,630 miles (4,235
kilometers) between Alaska
and Norway

Surface Temperature
Average low: 28°F,
   –2°C in January
Average high: 29°F,
   –1.5°C in July

▲ A seal swimming in the Arctic Ocean.

Chapter 1 ▶

THE OCEAN AT THE TOP OF THE WORLD

The Arctic Ocean lies at the top of the world. Most of its waters are within an imaginary line called the Arctic Circle.[1] The land and water here are known as the Arctic. Polar is another word used to describe the region because it is close to the North Pole. The North Pole lies near the

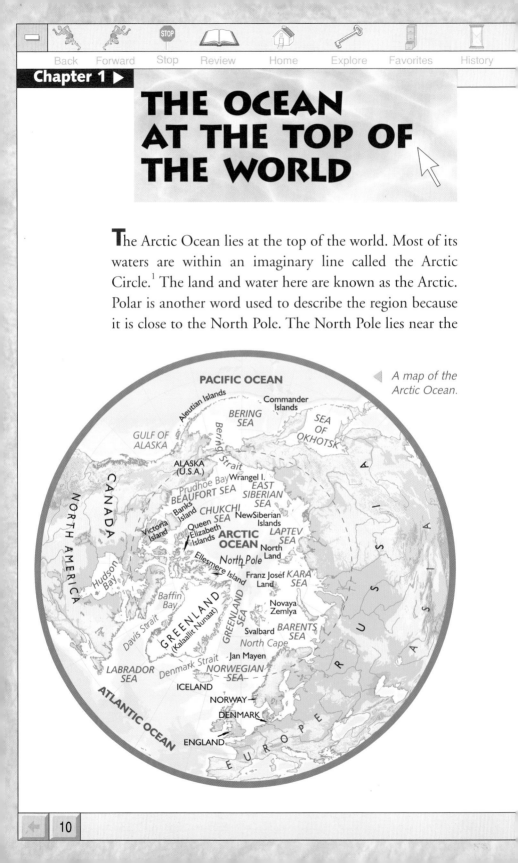

A map of the Arctic Ocean.

center of the Arctic Ocean. It represents the place where the earth's lines of longitude meet. There is no land at the North Pole, but the water here is always frozen.

The Arctic is the smallest ocean on earth. It covers about 5.5 million square miles (14 million square kilometers).[2] The northern coasts of Asia, Europe, and North America ring the Arctic Ocean. This ring is broken in only a few places.

One narrow strip of water runs between Asia and Alaska. It is called the Bering Strait. The Bering Strait links the Arctic Ocean to the Pacific Ocean. Opposite this, Arctic waters meet the Atlantic Ocean near the island of Greenland.

Islands sit along the edges of the surrounding continents. Some of the biggest ones are Ellesmere Island, Baffin Island, Iceland, Svalbard, and Novaya Zemlya. Greenland is the world's largest island. Much of it is covered with ice and glaciers.

The Arctic Ocean is divided into ten seas. Sea is sometimes used as another word for ocean. It can also mean a small part of an ocean. Some major Arctic seas are the Chukchi, Greenland, Barents, and the Beaufort Sea. Other large areas of water include Baffin Bay and Hudson Bay.

Some of the world's largest rivers empty into the Arctic. They bring freshwater into the salty ocean.

▶ Climate

Arctic temperatures are extremely cold. During July, the average temperature is 29°F (–1.5°C). In January, the average temperature drops to –28°F (–2°C).[3] Winds can make the air feel even colder. Sometimes it is so cold that humans cannot be outside, no matter how much clothing they are wearing.

These floes make up a sheet of ice covering the northern Bering Sea.

Ice

Cold temperatures keep much of the ocean frozen. Frozen seawater is called sea ice.

In the summer, ice extends from the North Pole towards the continents. It can be ten feet (three meters) thick. Summer ice covers about 3 million square miles (7.5 million square kilometers).[4] This area is about the same size as Australia. During these warmer months, open water is found near the continents.

Each winter, the sea ice doubles in size. It reaches land in many places.[5]

The ice is not one solid sheet, though. It is made up of several pieces separated by thinner ice or water. Each piece is called a *floe*.

Water under the floes moves and breaks the ice on top. So do strong winds. Sea ice that is broken apart then crushed back together again is called pack ice. Pack ice forms around the edges of floes. It can be six feet (two meters) thick.

Sometimes water and wind fold the ice over onto itself. This makes a pressure ridge. Pressure ridges are sometimes as tall as a two-story house. All of the cracking and shifting ice can be noisy. Roaring and grinding sounds are common around the Arctic.

▲ The position and brightness of the sun can make an iceberg look blue, pink, gray, or green.

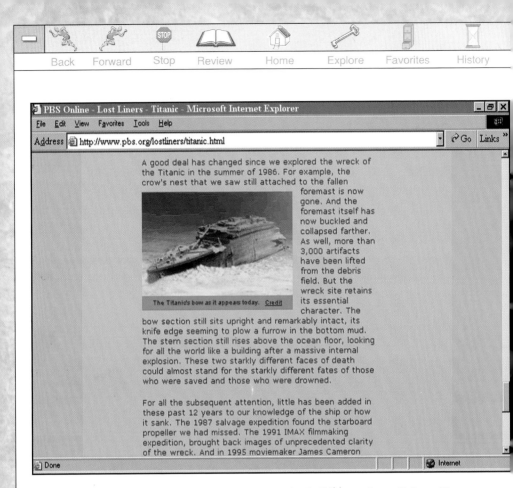

A good deal has changed since we explored the wreck of the Titanic in the summer of 1986. For example, the crow's nest that we saw still attached to the fallen foremast is now gone. And the foremast itself has now buckled and collapsed farther. As well, more than 3,000 artifacts have been lifted from the debris field. But the wreck site retains its essential character. The bow section still sits upright and remarkably intact, its knife edge seeming to plow a furrow in the bottom mud. The stern section still rises above the ocean floor, looking for all the world like a building after a massive internal explosion. These two starkly different faces of death could almost stand for the starkly different fates of those who were saved and those who were drowned.

For all the subsequent attention, little has been added in these past 12 years to our knowledge of the ship or how it sank. The 1987 salvage expedition found the starboard propeller we had missed. The 1991 IMAX filmmaking expedition, brought back images of unprecedented clarity of the wreck. And in 1995 moviemaker James Cameron

The Titanic's bow as it appears today. Credit

▲ The Titanic *stayed afloat for two-and-a-half hours after colliding with an iceberg that had drifted south from the Arctic Ocean. Damage done to the great ship caused it to sink to where it now sits—at the bottom of the Atlantic Ocean.*

Another kind of ice is found in the ocean. It is called glacier ice. Glacier ice is frozen freshwater that has broken off glaciers on land. These chunks are called icebergs.

Icebergs can be several miles long and hundreds of feet tall. Yet only a small part of any iceberg lies above the water. The largest portion is hidden under the sea. Icebergs can look like castles with towers and spires. They can be pink, blue, gray, or green depending on the sun's position and brightness.

Many icebergs stay in the Arctic for years. Others float into warmer waters and melt. In 1912, one Arctic iceberg floated into the Atlantic Ocean and was struck by a ship called the *Titanic*.[6]

Kinds of Water

The percentage of salt in water is called its salinity. The salinity of Arctic water is different in different places. This is because the ocean is often thawing or freezing.

As ocean water freezes, the salt inside it sinks. When the ice melts, the water has less salt than deeper water. This makes it lighter, so it floats on top of the heavier, saltier water. This top layer is called Arctic surface water. It extends to a depth of 150 feet (46 meters).

The water at the bottom of the Arctic Ocean is the saltiest of all. Arctic bottom water lies from 2,800 feet (850 meters) deep to the bottom of the sea. Its average temperature is 30°F (–1°C). Water usually freezes before it gets this cold. Saltwater does not freeze as quickly as water without salt.

The water between the two layers is either Pacific water or Atlantic water. Currents bring water from both oceans into the Arctic Ocean.

Currents

Currents are like rivers in the ocean. They move in a constant and regular pattern. Several currents flow below Arctic ice.

Two main currents bring water into the Arctic Ocean. The first flows northward between Iceland and Norway. It brings water from the Atlantic Ocean into the Arctic. The second major current brings Pacific water into the Arctic through the Bering Strait.

A third important current takes water out of the Arctic Ocean. It flows south along Greenland into the Atlantic Ocean.

▶ The Sky Above

The Arctic is tilted toward the sun for about half of each year. During this time, the sun never sets above the North Pole. It is a time of constant daylight. For the next six months, though, the Arctic is tilted away from the sun. At this time, the sun never rises at the North Pole. It is dark all day and night.

Another unique event over Arctic waters is the *aurora borealis*, or northern lights. These are glowing green, red, or purple lights that appear in the sky. They occur when electrical particles from the sun get trapped in the earth's magnetic field. The northern lights can be seen for thousands of miles. This natural light show is just one of the things that makes the Arctic Ocean a fascinating place.

Chapter 2

NATURAL RESOURCES

People have lived in the area around the Arctic Ocean since prehistoric times. As a group, they are often called Eskimos. Yet each group of people usually prefers to be referred to by a more specific name. For example, the people in northern Alaska are the Inupiat. The Inuit are from Canada. Saamis live in northern Europe. There are other groups as well.

Each group speaks its own language and has its own culture. All groups have one thing in common. That is that they use natural resources carefully.

▲ The Arctic's native peoples have survived since prehistoric times, relying a great deal on the ocean to provide what they need.

Fish was once a major part of the diets of these native groups. They also ate seals, walrus, and whales. Arctic people used every part of any animal they killed. The hide was used for clothing, boats, and shelters. The animal's fat was used for cooking and heating. Arctic people even used animal tusks to carve utensils or pieces of art.

Some descendants of these people still practice the customs of their ancestors. They depend on ocean fish and sea mammals for their food. Others who live near the ocean also depend on its sea life. Many earn a living fishing. Some of the world's best fishing waters are in the Barents and Bering seas.[1] Much of the catch is sold to people in the Arctic. Much more is shipped elsewhere. In fact, each year Arctic waters provide one tenth of all the fish eaten in the world.[2]

Energy

The Arctic Ocean is also an important source of oil and natural gas. These fuels are used to heat homes and power engines. There are oil deposits under the sea floor near Canada and Russia.

In addition, oil is pumped from under the Beaufort Sea near Prudhoe Bay, Alaska. This oil is sent through an eight-hundred-mile-long pipeline to Valdez, Alaska. Oil tankers at Valdez take the oil to the United States mainland. Alaska supplies the United States with one fourth of all the oil it uses each year.[3]

Sand, Gravel, and Metal

Tons of sand and gravel are also taken from the bottom of the Arctic Ocean. They are major ingredients in cement.

In addition, there is iron, copper, lead, and uranium on the Arctic floor. However, the cold and ice make it

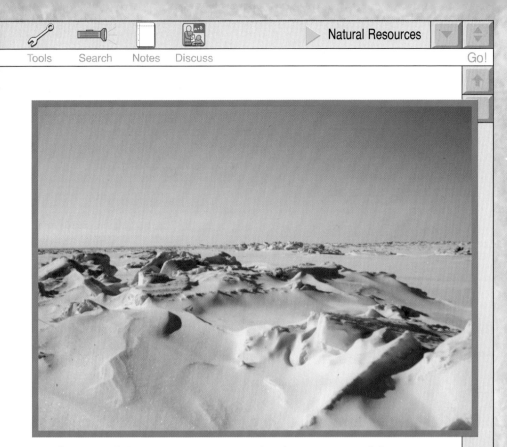

▲ *Much of the Arctic Ocean is covered with sea ice most of the year. However, some experts say that global warming has made sea ice three to six feet thinner than normal, a 40 percent decrease in the total amount of Arctic sea ice.*

difficult to mine them. Therefore, most of these metals lie untouched.

▷ Transportation

The Arctic Ocean provides two important sea routes for moving goods around the world. The first is the Northwest Passage. Ships using it travel north from Greenland, then west through the islands of northern Canada. Once they reach Alaska, they pass through the Bering Strait to the Pacific Ocean. This passage is free of ice only four months each year.

The second ocean route is the Northern Sea Route. To use it, ships sail around the northern coast of Europe. They then travel around Arctic Asia and through the Bering Strait to the Pacific Ocean.

Both routes are difficult. Airplanes often guide ships around the ice. Sometimes icebreakers are needed. Icebreakers are ships with thick hulls and powerful engines that can plow through ice.

In spite of difficulties, tons of products are shipped through the Arctic each year. These routes are thousands of miles shorter than other routes that would avoid the area. They save both time and money.

The Arctic also provides the shortest air route between many places in North America, Europe, and Asia. Airplanes fly over the ocean every day.

Military Importance

Canada, the United States, and Russia use Arctic islands and coasts for military bases. These bases help each country protect itself from any attack coming across Arctic waters. One such base is the Eielson Air Force Base in Alaska.

Weather Forecaster

Perhaps the Arctic's most important use is as a weather forecaster. The Arctic Oscillation is a predictable weather pattern. When it makes Arctic weather especially cold, weather in Europe and the eastern United States is especially warm. When temperatures in the Arctic are warmer than usual, temperatures in Europe and the eastern United States are colder than usual. Each swing of the oscillation lasts about ten years.[4]

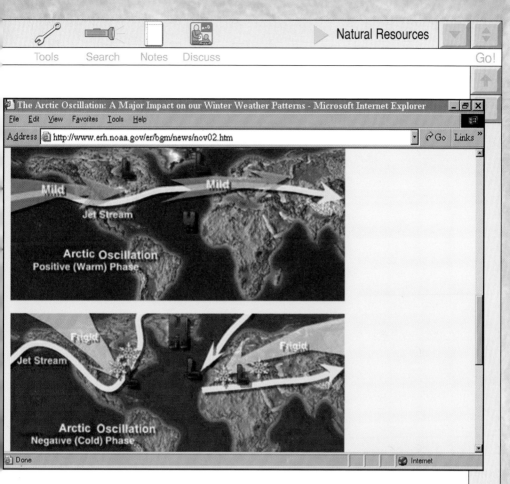

▲ *When the Arctic Oscillation is positive, little snow and mild temperatures are experienced in the United States. When the Arctic Oscillation is negative, this results in heavy snowfall and cold weather.*

More importantly, scientists believe that the Arctic climate is getting warmer. This change could trigger storms, droughts, and floods all over the world. The warming could kill large numbers of plants and animals. Experts from many countries are working together to study the impact of Arctic weather. They hope to predict future climate changes so people can prepare for them.[5]

THE OCEAN BELOW

The Arctic Ocean is the shallowest ocean on Earth. Its average depth is 3,665 feet (1,117 meters).[1] The ocean bottom slopes gently from the land into the sea. This slope is called the continental shelf. All oceans have a continental shelf. The Arctic's shelf is especially wide. In some places it stretches for 1,000 miles (1,600 kilometers). Most of it is less than 500 feet (150 meters) deep.

At the end of the shelf, steep cliffs plunge downward. Narrow canyons cut through these cliffs. They are known as submarine canyons.

▶ Abyss

The floor at the bottom of the cliffs is the deepest part of the ocean. It lies from 10,000 to 12,000 feet (3,000 to 3,600 meters) below the surface. This is called the abyss. The deepest point in the Arctic abyss is 15,272 feet (4,655 meters) deep. It is named Fram Basin.[2]

▶ Mountains In the Sea

Several mountain ranges lie at the bottom of the abyss. One is the Lomonosov Ridge. The Lomonosov Ridge runs between Greenland and Siberia. It is nearly 1,000 miles (1,600 kilometers) long.

A deep basin lies on each side of the Lomonosov Ridge. The basin on the European and Asian side is called the Eurasia Basin. The basin on the North American side is called the Amerasia Basin.[3] Water at the bottom of the

Towering Mountains

Towering mountain ranges known as submarine ridges run through and around the Arctic Ocean basin. These ridges were formed when the earth's continental plates slowly separated, leaving gaps in the earth's crust. Molten rock moved up into the gap, forming a new part of the ocean floor - the ridges that now divide the Arctic Basin into many sub-basins. Some of these submarine ridges run in straight lines for over 1,500 kilometres, and are steep and narrow, having widths of only about 200 metres. A number of peaks and valleys occur along the ridges, with crests rising to within a kilometre of the ocean surface.

The central submarine ridge, the Lomonosov Ridge, runs 1,770 kilometres from Ellesmere Island to the New Siberian Islands, a distance equivalent to that separating Toronto from Halifax! This ridge divides the Arctic Basin into two main basins: the Eurasian Basin - also called the Nansen Basin, and the Amerasian Basin - also known as the North American or Hyperborean Basin. Within the Eurasian Basin, the Nansen-Gakkel Ridge runs from east to west, dividing the basin into the northern Fram Basin, and the southern Nansen Basin. The geographic North Pole is located over the floor of the Fram Basin. The Nansen Basin is the smallest of the sub-basins within the Arctic Ocean. The Barents Abyssal Plain, an incredibly flat expanse, is located in the heart of the Fram Basin, at depths of over

Address: http://www.aquatic.uoguelph.ca/oceans/ArticOceanWeb/Features/Toweringmts.htm

The ridges of the deep ocean separate the basin into at least 4 different parts

▲ When the earth's continental plates shifted, they left gaps in the ocean floor. Molten rock then pushed through to create underwater mountain ridges. These ridges separate the sub-basins that make up the Arctic Basin.

basins is very cold and still. No water flows into or out of them.

A shorter mountain range, called the Alpha Ridge, runs through the Amerasia Basin. A third chain of mountains lies in the Eurasian Basin. It is part of a range that winds its way through every ocean on Earth. This long chain is known as the mid-ocean ridge.

The mid-ocean ridge has a different name in every ocean it passes through. In the Arctic, it is known as Gakkel Ridge. It is east of the Lomonosov Ridge. Gakkel Ridge is about 1,800 miles (2,900 kilometers) long.[4]

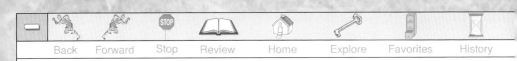
The mid-ocean ridge is a place where powerful forces inside the earth are splitting the earth's crust apart. Magma (liquid molten rock) below the crust rises and fills the gash. It then cools and becomes new crust. This is called sea floor spreading.

Sea floor spreading along the Gakkel Ridge is slower than spreading anywhere else in the world. Each year, the ridge only spreads by about the width of your little finger.[5]

Hot Vents

Scientists have recently found hot vents in the Arctic. A hot vent occurs at a crack in the earth's crust. Water seeps into the crack and mixes with hot gases and minerals inside the earth. The water is then shot into the ocean like a geyser. Sometimes this water is as hot as 700°F (371°C).[6]

Most Arctic vents lie along the Gakkel Ridge. This is where cracks in the crust are most common.

Volcanoes

Several volcanoes also lie along the Gakkel Ridge. They, too, occur where there is a crack in the crust. Volcanoes form when gases and minerals from inside the earth mix with water and mud on the ocean floor. This mixture oozes and bubbles around the crack. Arctic volcanoes are sometimes called mud volcanoes.[7]

The best-explored Arctic volcano is near the Barents Sea. It is called the Haakon Mosby mud volcano. The volcano is about one-half mile (one kilometer) wide but only 6 feet (2 meters) high.

Scientists once thought that the Arctic floor was bare and still. However, the recent discovery of hot vents and volcanoes is changing their ideas.

ARCTIC LIFE

Every ocean contains plankton. Plankton are plants and animals that drift about with the currents. There are two kinds of plankton: phytoplankton and zooplankton.

Types of Plankton

Phytoplankton are plants. Some are so small they can only be seen with a microscope. Phytoplankton use the sun's energy to make food. This is called photosynthesis. Photosynthesis is how plants on land survive as well.

Phytoplankton are rare in the Arctic Ocean during the winter. These months are too dark for plants to make food. In the summer, however, many days have twenty-four hours of sunlight. During these months, Arctic waters are thick with phytoplankton.

Some phytoplankton live under the ice. They lie dormant (inactive) all winter. In spring they bloom and spread to the edge of the ice. Some of these plants can grow several feet long.[1]

The plankton can also be tiny animals. They are called zooplankton. Some are microscopic, but others can be seen with the eye. Zooplankton eat phytoplankton. In addition, big zooplankton eat little zooplankton.

Zooplankton live in the areas of open water. They also live under sea ice and eat the plants above them.

Some plankton even live in the sea ice. They inhabit tiny pockets of water that form when the water freezes.

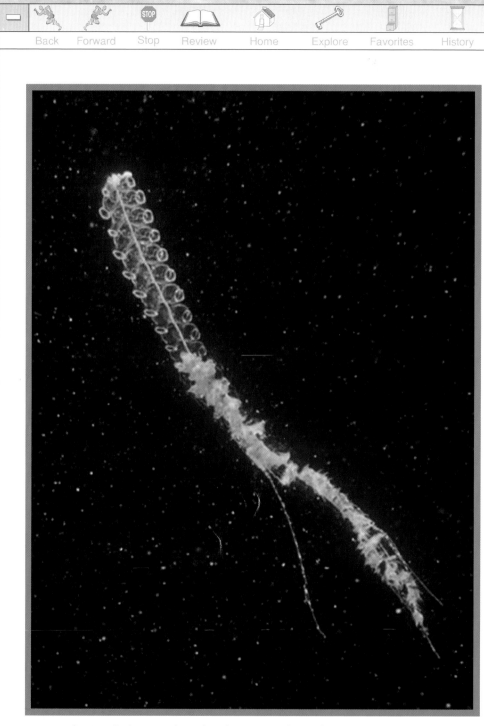

▲ Zooplankton, such as the physonect siphonophore shown here, exist in every ocean, including the Arctic Ocean.

Over a large area of ice, these pockets become a system of tunnels. The tunnels are home to many different kinds of plankton.[2] Fish and other marine life depend on plankton for food.

Fish

The most common Arctic fish is the cod. Arctic cod feed on plankton that live in and under the ice. Other Arctic fish include the capelin, herring, and halibut. In addition, salmon live near rivers that empty into the sea. They travel up the rivers each year to lay their eggs.

There are fewer kinds of fish in Arctic waters than in any other ocean. For example, while hundreds of different

▲ *Cod is the most common fish in the Arctic Ocean. This open-mouthed cod is ready for market.*

▲ *Plankton are eaten by fish that are then eaten by seals, like the one shown above. This is a small part of the Arctic food chain.*

sharks live elsewhere, only one lives in the Arctic. It is the Greenland shark.[3]

▶ Mammals of the Sea

Several mammals, though, have learned to survive the cold Arctic waters. Many kinds of whales inhabit its waters. All have thick layers of blubber, or fat. The blubber acts like a coat to keep them warm.

Many Arctic whales are baleen whales. Baleen whales do not have teeth. Instead, they have hundreds of thin plates that hang from the roofs of their mouths. These thin plates are called baleen.

To eat, baleen whales gulp seawater. As the water runs out of their mouths, plankton gets trapped in the baleen. Baleen whales survive solely on plankton.

The humpback whale is a baleen whale. So is the blue whale. The blue whale is the largest animal on Earth. It can grow to be one hundred feet (thirty meters) long. This is almost as long as three school buses.

Both the humpback and blue whale are migrators. This means they do not live in one place. Migrating whales live in the Arctic during the summer. Each winter they swim to warmer oceans.

Some baleen whales stay in the Arctic year-round. The bowhead, for example, lives in small groups that never leave the Arctic. Bowheads have two blowholes near the top of their heads.

Two other whales stay in Arctic waters all year long. They are the narwhal and beluga whales. Both grow to only 15 feet (4.5 meters). They are toothed whales. Toothed whales have teeth and eat fish.

Narwhals live in groups. Male narwhals grow a spiraling tusk 8 feet (2.5 meters) long.

Adult belugas are all white. They are the only whales who can turn their heads to look around. Belugas make chirping and whistling noises.

Mammals of the Land and Sea

Some Arctic mammals live on the land and in the sea. One is the seal. Many different seals live in the Arctic. The most common are the spotted seal, the harp seal, the ribbon seal, and the bearded seal. All have hair on their bodies and thick layers of blubber to keep them warm.

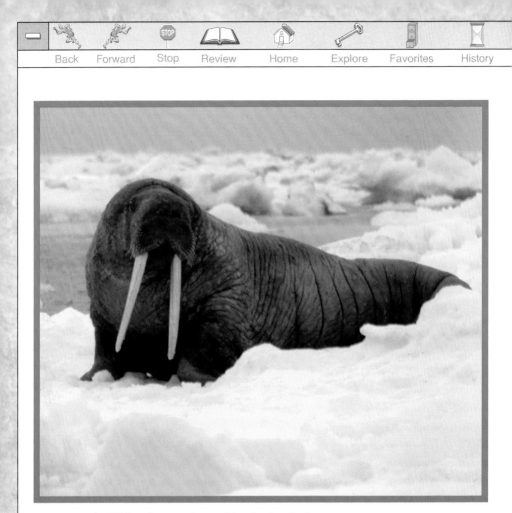

▲ *Walrus live on pieces of ice floating in the ocean.*

Seals spend much of their time in the water. They also enjoy resting on the ice.

Seals are excellent swimmers who eat fish. They swim under ice looking for food. Some can stay underwater for nearly an hour. When they need air, they find a hole in the ice and come up to breathe.

Walrus also live in the Arctic. A male walrus can grow to 12 feet (3.5 meters) long and weigh 3,000 pounds (1,360 kilograms). Walrus have ivory tusks that reach

3 feet (one meter) in length. They use them for fighting off predators and for climbing onto the ice.

Walrus live on large pieces of floating ice. Flippers make them good swimmers. They swim to the ocean bottom looking for clams, their favorite food.

Another mammal of the Arctic is the polar bear. Polar bears can grow 11 feet (3 meters) long and weigh more than 1,000 pounds (450 kilograms).

Polar bears have thick, white fur. This keeps them warm. It is also an excellent camouflage for hunting the seals they eat. Polar bears have a keen sense of smell. They can smell seal dens that are buried below snow.

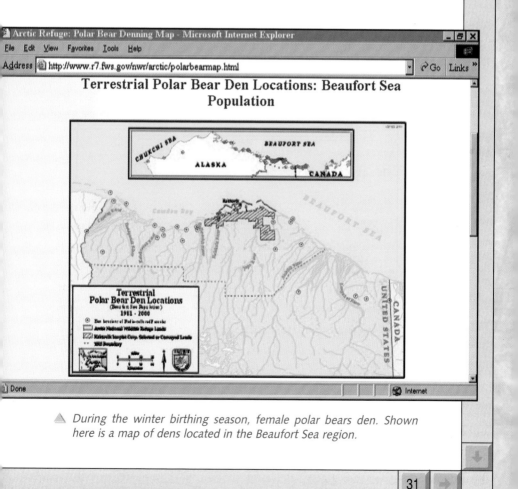

During the winter birthing season, female polar bears den. Shown here is a map of dens located in the Beaufort Sea region.

Polar bears are good swimmers. They sometimes catch seals in the water. They are smart, too. They wait at ice holes for seals to come up to breathe. Then they attack.

Bottom Dwellers

Animals live on the floor of the Arctic Ocean, too. Most do not have a backbone. Animals without backbones are called invertebrates. Some common Arctic invertebrates are sea anemones, sponges, sea stars, worms, clams, and crabs.[4]

There is even life around hot vents and volcanoes. A bacteria there makes food from the chemicals in the vented water. This process is called chemosynthesis. This bacteria is eaten by tube worms and other strange animals. These animals are eaten by fish called scalebelly eelpout. Greenland sharks eat the eelpout.[5]

Each life around these vents is an important part of its ecosystem. An ecosystem is a group of plants and animals that need each other to exist.

The Arctic Ecosystem

The Arctic Ocean is one huge ecosystem. These tiny plankton form the basis of this system. Without it, Arctic fish would have no food and would not survive. Without fish, whales and seals would go hungry. If there were no seals, polar bears could not live. Even the animals on the seafloor depend on the marine life above them. They eat the dead plants and animals that fall through the waters. If these bottom dwellers died, walrus would have no food.

Each life in any ecosystem is a vital link in its chain. If one link breaks, the whole chain falls apart.

EXPLORERS

The first to explore the Arctic Ocean were the Eskimo peoples. They came to the area thousands of years ago looking for food.

The next to visit the Arctic was a Greek man named Pytheas. He sailed on Arctic waters during the 300s B.C.[1] Pytheas returned to Greece and told others about the frozen sea he had found. The Greeks named the sea "Arktos," meaning bear. This is what they called the Big Dipper, a constellation in the northern sky.

Viking sailors from Denmark came to the Arctic during the A.D. 800s. They sailed along its southern edge looking for new lands to settle.

▷ Northwest Passage

During the 1500s, the Europeans searched the Arctic for a sea route to Asia. They hoped to find a shorter way than sailing around South America or Africa. One possible route might be to head west along northern North America. This became known as the search for a Northwest Passage.

In 1610, Henry Hudson of Ireland searched for the waterway. He thought he had discovered it when he sailed between Baffin Island and Canada. He had not. He had found a huge bay. It would later be named Hudson Bay.

In 1728, Vitus Bering of Denmark discovered a strip of water linking the Pacific Ocean to the Arctic. This strip

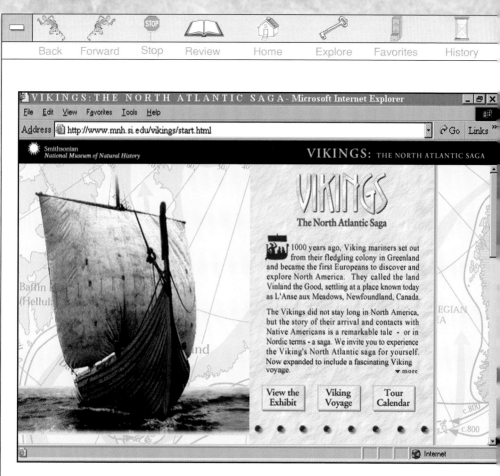

VIKINGS
The North Atlantic Saga

1000 years ago, Viking mariners set out from their fledgling colony in Greenland and became the first Europeans to discover and explore North America. They called the land Vinland the Good, settling at a place known today as L'Anse aux Meadows, Newfoundland, Canada.

The Vikings did not stay long in North America, but the story of their arrival and contacts with Native Americans is a remarkable tale - or in Nordic terms - a saga. We invite you to experience the Viking's North Atlantic saga for yourself. Now expanded to include a fascinating Viking voyage. ▼ more

| View the Exhibit | Viking Voyage | Tour Calendar |

▲ Vikings, Nordic-speaking peoples from southern Scandinavia, braved the extreme weather to settle both Greenland and Iceland.

is called the Bering Strait. Bering's discovery renewed hope that there was a Northwest Passage.

Sir Robert McClure of England set off to find the passage in 1850. He sailed east from Alaska to Banks Island. He then traveled by ship and sled to Baffin Bay. McClure completed his journey across the Arctic in four years. It was not the route he was looking for, however, because it was not completed by water alone.

A sea route through the islands of northern Canada was finally found in 1905. That year, Roald Amundsen of Norway completed his voyage from Greenland to the

Bering Strait. Finally, someone had found a true Northwest Passage.

Northeast Passage

Other explorers looked for an eastern route to Asia. In 1878, Adolf Nordenskjöld sailed along the northern coasts of Europe and Asia. He reached the Bering Strait in 1879. This made him the first person to navigate the Northeast Passage.

Nansen

While explorers looked for trade routes, Fridtjof Nansen of Norway wanted to know more about the ocean. How deep were its waters? Was there land under the ice?

Nansen built a special ship. It had rounded sides and looked something like an old bathtub. The front of the wooden ship was covered with sheets of iron. It needed to be strong enough to bear the ice of the north. Nansen called his ship the *Fram*.

Nansen stocked the *Fram* with enough food to last several years. In 1893, he set off for Arctic waters. The *Fram* was soon frozen in ice. As it drifted with the currents, Nansen studied the sea.

After two years of research, Nansen left his crew in charge. Then, he and a companion set off for the North Pole. Bad weather forced them to set up camp on an island in an area called Franz Josef Land.

In the meantime, the *Fram* broke free of the ice. The crew sailed it back to Norway. While they made their way home, Nansen and his friend were rescued by other explorers. They, too, headed for Norway. The *Fram* arrived home in June 1896. Nansen arrived one day later.[2]

Nansen's expedition found that the Arctic Ocean was warmer and deeper than anyone had thought. Most importantly, he proved that there was no continent lying under the Arctic ice.[3]

North Pole

During the early 1900s, adventurers tried to reach the North Pole. Severe weather kept most from getting there.

Then, American explorer Robert E. Peary set off on his third try. He claimed he reached the Pole in 1909. Today, some experts do not think Peary really made it to

the Pole. Others are sure he did.[4] This is a mystery that may never be solved.

The First Research Stations

In 1937, the Soviet Union built a small camp on ice near the North Pole. Four scientists lived there as the floe moved with the currents. They studied Arctic currents, ice, and water. Soon the Soviets set up

Robert Peary is credited with being the first American to reach the North Pole. On April 6, 1909, Peary and his team of five men, including an African American named Matthew Henson, planted an American flag in the ice at the location.

more stations. They also used airplanes and ships to study the Arctic.[5]

Research Today

Oceanographers in Canada, the United States, and other countries investigated the Arctic, too. Oceanographers are people who study the ocean.

In 1958, a United States submarine made the first sea voyage to the North Pole. It sailed under the ice.[6] The United States began using satellites to study the Arctic in the 1970s.

During the 1990s, United States' submarines cruised Arctic waters. Scientists inside were mapping the seafloor. Once in a while, a submarine would punch its way through the ice. Then scientists would have a look at the surface. These submarine missions doubled the amount of information known about the Arctic.[7]

In 1997, oceanographers repeated Nansen's experiment. They sailed an icebreaker into the ice and let it freeze. Then they studied the climate as the ship drifted in the water.

Other oceanographers wanted to know more about Arctic life. They took small submarines equipped with cameras and scientific instruments into the sea. These submarines are called submersibles. In 1997, researchers took a submersible to the Haakon Mosby mud volcano. There they studied the life around the vent.

In 2001, scientists sent remote-controlled submersibles into the Arctic. To their surprise, they found several hot vents and volcanoes along the Gakkel Ridge.[8]

Today, scientists know more about the Arctic region than ever before. Yet research continues, for it is still the least understood ocean.[9]

CURRENT ISSUES

Few people live around the Arctic Ocean. Yet, humans have polluted it. Three of the major causes of pollution in the Arctic are oil spills or leaks, runoff of chemicals used for agriculture, and nuclear waste.

▶ Types of Pollution

One of the most common pollutants is oil. Oil sometimes leaks from pipes or tanks onto Arctic lands. The leaked oil often ends up in rivers that run to the ocean. Sometimes

▲ *The pristine beauty of the Arctic Ocean and its surroundings have sometimes been tainted by human carelessness.*

▲ *Beluga whales can absorb chemicals such as DDT. This beluga looks as if it came up for a look around.*

ships leak oil directly into the sea. Oil kills plankton and other marine life.

Dangerous chemicals also pollute the ocean. One especially harmful chemical is DDT. Farmers use DDT to kill insects that ruin crops. Yet it harms other animals, too. Rains wash it from fields to rivers and then to the ocean. Some chemicals come from factories that dump their wastes straight into the sea.

Many animals, including beluga whales, polar bears, and seals, have absorbed these chemicals into their bodies. The chemicals cause health problems and prevent healthy reproduction. In addition, the chemicals are transferred to humans who eat the poisoned animals. The toxins affect human health, too.[1]

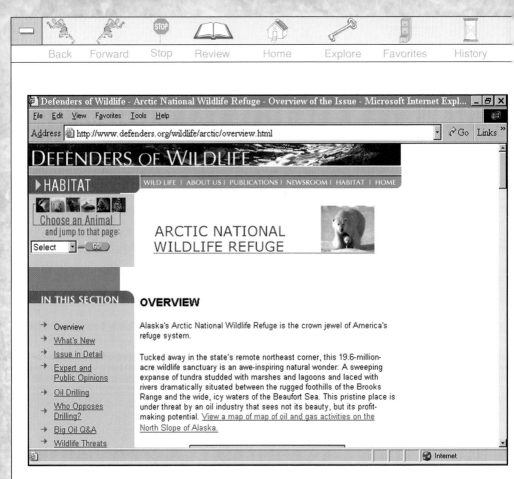

The Arctic National Wildlife Refuge, located in Alaska, protects 19.6 million acres of Arctic nature.

Another dangerous pollutant in the Arctic Ocean is nuclear waste. Some fell into the ocean when nuclear weapons were tested over it. Other nuclear waste has been dumped right into the sea.[2] Nuclear material kills animals. Furthermore, currents carry it to other oceans.

Overfishing and Hunting

Humans are also harming the Arctic Ocean by overfishing. Overfishing occurs when people catch too many fish in one area. Species that are overfished cannot reproduce fast enough to restock the waters.

Overfishing a species can lead to its depletion. It is then in danger of becoming extinct. Experts believe that nearly half of all marine fish caught for food are overfished.[3]

Animal numbers have also been harmed by hunting. Baby harp seals were once killed for their pure white fur. Narwhals were hunted for their tusks. Other whales have been hunted in such large numbers that they have become depleted.

Depletion harms more than one species. When one animal becomes scarce, another has less food. Soon this affects another animal, then another. The cycle continues until depletion of one species can eventually ruin an entire ecosystem.

▲ The effects of global warming on Arctic glacier ice have been less noticeable than in other places due to its colder temperatures. However, Arctic glacier ice has started thawing earlier than usual and large pieces have broken off.

Endangered Species

Animal and plant species in danger of becoming extinct are called endangered. Many countries protect these animals from being captured or killed.

Several Arctic species are endangered. Blue whales, bowhead whales, and belugas are all endangered. So are polar bears and the walrus. Protecting endangered species may build back their numbers.

Ozone

Another problem facing the Arctic is ozone depletion. Ozone is a form of oxygen that is natural in the earth's atmosphere. It mixes with other gases to form a layer of air called the ozone layer. This layer is twelve to twenty-five miles (twenty to forty kilometers) above the earth.

The ozone layer is the earth's natural sunscreen. It blocks ultraviolet (UV) rays that come from the sun. Without the ozone layer, too many UV rays would reach the earth. This would cause skin cancer in humans which could possibly lead to death. The rays would also kill plants and animals.

Scientists have found that the amount of ozone in the atmosphere is decreasing. One of the areas with the highest loss of ozone is over the Arctic. The layer there is only half the size it once was.[4]

Experts believe the ozone layer is broken down by chemicals called chloroflourocarbons (CFCs). CFCs were once used in cleaning, cooling, and other products packaged in spray cans. Using the products sent CFCs into the air and destroyed ozone. In 1990, several nations stopped using CFCs. Scientists hope this will help the ozone layer recover.[5]

Global Warming

Climate change is another problem in the Arctic region. Temperatures all around the globe are getting warmer. This is called global warming. At the rate temperatures are rising, many scientists predict the earth's temperature will warm nearly two degrees by 2050.[6] This does not seem

The polar bear is greatly affected by changes in the Arctic. The bear depends on sea ice, which is being thinned by warmer temperatures, as well as the food the ocean provides, which is becoming toxic due to humans. Oil exploration also disturbs this animal's habitat.

like much. Yet, it could completely change the climate in the Northern Hemisphere.[7]

Furthermore, it looks as though global warming is melting Arctic ice. The ice has thinned by about four feet since the 1960s.[8] This is a serious threat to all Arctic life. Seals, polar bears, and walrus spend much of their lives on the ice. Cod and other fish eat the plankton that live in and under ice. In fact, the entire ecosystem of the Arctic depends on ice. Without it, all species would suffer.

Scientists are trying to learn why the earth is warming. They know that carbon dioxide keeps heat from escaping the earth. Without this heat trap, the world would be extremely cold. Too much carbon dioxide, though, makes the earth too warm.

Fuels such as coal and gas release carbon dioxide into the air. At the start of the twenty-first century, there were more cars, trucks, and factories on our planet than ever before. Each of those things release carbon dioxide into the atmosphere as it burns fuel. This adds to the amount already there. Many scientists think this is why the earth is warming.

Others disagree. They think that global warming is a natural occurrence. They believe that the earth's climate has been changing since the beginning of time. Global warming, they say, is a normal part of a natural cycle.[9]

It may be too soon to know why global warming is happening. One thing is certain, though. If humans do not take better care of the Arctic Ocean, one of the most fascinating environments on earth will be changed forever.

Chapter Notes

Chapter 1. The Ocean at the Top of the World

1. Central Intelligence Agency, *World Factbook 2002* (Washington, D.C.: Brassey's, 2002), p. 20.

2. Ibid.

3. *Antarctica and the Arctic: The Complete Encyclopedia* (Ontario: Firefly Books Ltd., 2001), p. 52.

4. I. A. Melnikov, *The Arctic Sea Ice Ecosystem* (The Netherlands: Overseas Publishers Association, 1997), p. vii.

5. Ibid.

6. Trevor Day, *Oceans* (New York: Facts On File, 1999), p. 12.

Chapter 2. Natural Resources

1. *Antarctica and the Arctic: The Complete Encyclopedia* (Ontario: Firefly Books Ltd., 2001), p. 535.

2. Trevor Day, *Oceans* (New York: Facts On File, 1999), p. 13.

3. Ibid.

4. Glenn Hodges, "Arctic Submarine," *National Geographic*, March 2000, p. 38.

5. Paul R. Pinet, *Invitation to Oceanography* (Sudbury, Mass: Jones and Bartlett Publishers, 2000), p. 503.

Chapter 3. The Ocean Below

1. Trevor Day, *Oceans* (New York: Facts On File, 1999), p. 12.

2. Central Intelligence Agency, *World Factbook 2002* (Washington, D.C.: Brassey's, 2002), p. 21.

3. John H. Steele, editor in chief, *Encyclopedia of Ocean Sciences* (San Diego: Academic Press, 2001), p. 177.

4. S. Perkins, "Northern Vents," *Science News*, January 18, 2003, p. 37.

5. Ibid.

6. Richard Ellis, *Encyclopedia of the Sea* (New York: Alfred A. Knopf, 2000), p. 161.

7. Peter Vogt, "Vent and Seep Communities on the Arctic Seafloor," *Arctic Theme Page*, n.d., <http://www.arctic.noaa.gov/essay_vogt.html> (July 31, 2003).

Chapter 4. Arctic Life

1. I. A. Melnikov, *The Arctic Sea Ice Ecosystem* (The Netherlands: Overseas Publishers Association, 1997), p. 73.

2. Christopher Krembs and Jody Deming, "Is There Life in a Desert of Ice?" *Arctic Theme Page*, n.d., <http://www.arctic.noaa.gov/essay_krembsdeming.html> (July 31, 2003).

3. *Antarctica and the Arctic: The Complete Encyclopedia* (Ontario: Firefly Books Ltd., 2001), p. 363.

4. Bodil Bluhm and Katrin Iken, "Life on the Arctic Deep Sea Floor," *Ocean Explorer/Explorations*, May 2, 2003, <http://oceanexplorer.noaa.gov/explorations/02arctic/background/benthos/benthos.html> (July 31, 2003).

5. Peter Vogt, "Vent and Seep Communities on the Arctic Seafloor," *Arctic Theme Page*, n.d., <http://www.arctic.noaa.gov/essay_vogt.html> (July 31, 2003).

Chapter 5. Explorers

1. Paul R. Pinet, *Invitation to Oceanography* (Mass.: Jones and Bartlett Publishers, 2000), p. 8.

2. *Antarctica and the Arctic: The Complete Encyclopedia* (Ontario: Firefly Books Ltd., 2001), p. 511.

3. Steve Kershaw, *Oceanography: An Earth Science Perspective* (United Kingdom: Stanley Thornes Ltd., 2000), p. 14.

4. Richard Ellis, *Encyclopedia of the Sea* (New York: Alfred A. Knopf, 2000), pp. 250–251.

5. Don Belt, "An Arctic Breakthrough," *National Geographic*, February 1997, p. 44.

6. Pinet, p. 13.

7. Glenn Hodges, "Arctic Submarine," *National Geographic*, March 2000, p. 35.

8. S. Perkins, "Northern Vents," *Science News*, January 18, 2003, p. 37.

9. Hodges, p. 41.

Chapter 6. Current Issues

1. Mark Nuttall and Terry V. Callaghan, ed., *The Arctic: Environment, People, Policy* (The Netherlands: Overseas Publishers Association, 2000), p. 586.

2. Ibid., pp. 577–578.

3. Tom Garrison, *Essentials of Oceanography* (Calif.: Brooks/Cole, 2001), p. 302.

4. Ibid., p. 312.

5. Ibid., p. 313.

6. Ibid., p. 314.

7. Paul R. Pinet, *Invitation to Oceanography* (Mass.: Jones and Bartlett Publishers, 2000), pp. 502–503.

8. Glenn Hodges, "Arctic Submarine," *National Geographic*, March 2000, p. 35.

9. Harold V. Thurman and Alan P. Trujillo, *Essentials of Oceanography* (New Jersey: Prentice Hall, 2002), p. 187.

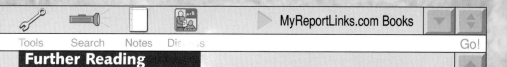
Further Reading

Calvert, Patricia. *Robert E. Peary: To the Top of the World.* Tarrytown, N.Y.: Marshall Cavendish Corporation, 2001.

Dudley, William. *Endangered Oceans.* Farmington Hills, Mich.: Gale Group, 1999.

Fowler, Allan. *Living in the Arctic.* Danbury, Conn.: Children's Press, 2000.

Grupper, Jonathan. *Destination, Polar Regions.* Washington, D.C.: National Geographic Society, 1999.

Littlefield, Cindy A. *Awesome Ocean Science: Investigating the Secrets of the Underwater World.* Charlotte, Vt.: Williamson Publishers, 2002.

Litwin, Laura Baskes. *Matthew Henson: Co-Discoverer of the North Pole.* Berkeley Heights, N.J.: Enslow Publishers, Inc., 2001.

Prevost, John F. *Arctic Ocean.* Edina, Minn.: ABDO Publishing Company, 2000.

Rootes, David. *The Arctic.* Minneapolis, Minn.: Lerner Publishing Group, 1996.

Staff. *Arctic Peoples: The Hands-On Approach to History.* Princeton, N.J.: Two-Can Publishers, 2000.

Turk, Jon. *Cold Oceans: Adventures in Kayak, Rowboat, and Dogsled.* New York: Harper Trade, 1999.

Voglino, Alex et al. *Ocean Environments.* Austin, Tex.: Raintree Publishers, 1998.

Young, Karen Romano. *Arctic Investigations: Exploring the Frozen Ocean.* Austin, Tex.: Raintree Publishers, 1999.

Index